IMAGES
OF GOD

IMAGES OF GOD

SIXTY REFLECTIONS OF SPIRITUAL BELIEFS

ADAM GAYNOR

HAZELDEN®

INFORMATION & EDUCATIONAL SERVICES

50th

1949-1999

HAZELDEN

HAZELDEN

Center City, Minnesota 55012-0176

1-800-328-0094

1-651-213-4590 (fax)

www.hazelden.org

Library of Congress Cataloging-in-Publication Data

Gaynor, Adam.

Images of God: sixty reflections of spiritual

beliefs/Adam Gaynor.

p. c.m.

ISBN 1-56838-322-3

1. God. I. Title

BL205.G35 1999

291.4'32—DC21   98-55294

CIP

03 02 01 00 99   6 5 4 3 2 1

Cover design by Mimi Dutta

Interior design/typesetting by Theresa Gedig

❊

To my grandfather Captain Herbert C. Cohen,

this book is dedicated to you, Pop.

CONTENTS

Mystics, prophets, and visionaries of the different religions have realized that the formless God can assume form in the human imagination. In the absence of all form there is no God to worship, but any God that is captured in a specific form is an idol and not the God who should be worshiped. Within the imagination, however, God is both present in and absent from the image. God is without image, yet appears in the human mind by means of multiple, varied images. No one sees God in exactly the same way.

This point is illustrated by one of the prominent motifs in Sufism, the mystical tradition of Islam: the paradoxical notion of the veil. The veil hides the very face that it also reveals; indeed, it reveals by veiling, and it veils by revealing. The face of God, which is in and of itself invisible, appears only through a multiplicity of veils, yet it is through these veils that the face of God is concealed. To imagine that one can see the face of God without any veil is the greatest of veils. One can see the face only through the veil; one uncovers the truth by covering it up.

Through this powerful symbol, Sufism has articulated an insight shared by the major religious traditions: God is beyond image—even beyond the image of God—but it is precisely because God is imageless that so many images of God can be seen. The hiddenness of God alone makes the disclosure of God possible. Indeed, mystics through the generations have acknowledged time and again that God is nowhere more present than in the place from which God is absent.

The great Hasidic master Nahman of Bratslav spoke of types of concealment of God: The first consists of God being hidden from human beings. Although this is a difficult situation, it allows one to search for God since one is aware of the fact that God is hidden. However, there is a second concealment in which God's concealment is itself concealed. Since one does not know that God is concealed, there appears to be no way to find God. God simply seems not to be there, but even in this case of concealment within concealment, God is manifest. The presence of God actually is most visible when there is nothing to see.

The faces portrayed in *Images of God* reveal that each person's face is a mirror in which God appears, a mirror of the soul that bears the imprint of the invisible God. Perhaps there is no better way to have a vision of God than by looking in the eyes of our fellow human beings. In the gleam of joy, the wince of pain, the gaze of desire, there dwells the image of the imageless God.

Elliot R. Wolfson
Director of Religious Study
New York University

This book was made possible with the love and help of my parents, siblings, siblings-in-law, and the following people: John Sann, James Apt, Seymour Gaynor, Tracy E. Heston, Elsa Li' Donni, Miriam Michaels, Macall Polay, and Goldalee M. Semel.

I extend my thanks to my editor, Betty Christiansen; my art director, David Spohn; my executive editor, Becky Post; my publisher, Clay Garner; my manuscript editor, Kathryn Kjorlien; and my agent, William Clark.

I extend my special thanks to Goldalee M. Semel and Heidi Arbogast for their help in writing the introduction.

I am also very thankful to the following people who also offered their support:

Kate Lehman	Ruth Samuels	Justine and Frankie Kerner
Janice and Tom Sann	Judy Cordo	Jennifer and Danny Moyer
Alice Genese	David Biton	Lavinia Leopold
Cameron and Sophie Frostbaum	Jaclyn Piudik	Edie Constantine
Chloe Gaynor	Suzanne Zenkel	Lois Zenkel
Michelle Eabry	Francine Halvorgen	Willis Hartshorn
Karyn Kuhl	Uncle Alan	Denise Leong
The Michaels Family	Kim Miller	Rebecca Hood
Amber Clapp	Samantha Brooks	John Kearney
Robert Feldman	Stacey Kalberman	Potri Ranka Manis

I also thank those who were photographed but not chosen for the final selection:

Amy	David	Eva	Kenryu	Mei-Suan	Sandra
Anna	Deborah	Francisco	Kimberly	Michael	Stella
Anna-Nina	Dorothy	James	Lina	Pamela	Susan
Audrey	Dot	Jamie	Lou	Porter	Sutham
Bob	Elsa	John	Louis	Rodney	Tennison
Carol	Erika	Kathleen	Mary	Sakaye	Teresa

I am grateful to Brave New Words and Catherine Revland for transcribing the interviews.

Images of God invites people of various beliefs and religions to reflect on the question "What does God mean to you?" There are nearly six billion people in the world today, and within this lies an equal number of interpretations to be shared and contemplated. How does one come to the meaning of God or to a spiritual life? How do we have faith in the midst of a troubled society? Why does one person denounce the existence of God after the death of her son, while another holds the belief that the same God causes human loss and suffering in order to take people to a better place? An inquiry of this paradox links us, even within our differences. *Images of God* offers an intimate study of people's beliefs by allowing various interpretations to resonate as we move between each image and story.

One of the first questions I pondered when I was a child, and one that still remains relatively elusive to me, is whether there is a power that exists that is greater than myself. When I first began my recovery from substance abuse, the most difficult issue to cope with was the insistence that I place my belief in a force outside of myself. It was hard to separate the concept of God from the concept of a Higher Power. I was not yet comfortable accepting myself. But the more I became comfortable with myself and involved in my recovery, the closer I came to accepting and the more intrigued I became by the probability of a God truly existing. I also

realized several other important truths, namely, that all people grow up asking similar questions: "Where do we come from?" "Why are we here?" "While we're here, what is our purpose?" "What happens after we die?" I, like many people, torment myself by confronting questions I cannot answer, yet there are others who are not tormented by the unanswerable. There are still others who retreat into the comfort of their unquestioned beliefs. And I hope, as our depth of understanding evolves, so does our perception of the world as we begin to search for answers beyond and within ourselves.

During my childhood my family belonged to a Jewish synagogue, and we practiced various traditional observances and rituals. This might lead one to conclude that I had a belief in God since I studied his word; however, during my childhood and even after my bar mitzvah, my image of God was as mysterious to me as my reading of the haftarah and as fictitious as the Curious George books that lined my bedroom shelves. When I was young, I remember poring over books of old photographs and having so many questions. Turn-of-the-century portraits were particularly troubling to me, for there seemed to be a silence behind weathered faces and stern expressions. I studied these images for hours, inspired by the butterfly-wing-like frailness of each photograph, its place in time, and the dramatic hardness captured within the subjects' gazes. Was the look that I saw in their eyes deceptive or descriptive? For me, these portraits held God's presence, but they also held a beckoning silence from those long gone, which I wanted to break in order to better communicate with them. I wanted to know their thoughts; I wanted their faith, for it belonged to a place I could only imagine, and I felt this somehow was linked to God. As I continue to reflect on this fascination as an adult, I see the presence of photography connected to this quest. I am compelled by what I feel may exist, that is, what I know to be real and what is at the same time unknowable or, at least at this point in time, just beyond my grasp. As Roland Barthes once wrote, "The photograph of the missing being . . . will touch me like the delayed rays of a star."

For one of the subjects in *Images of God*, a boy named Jesse, God becomes fantastical, visualized in a magical sense: "God floats by the side of earth. When his skin falls off, he has it in his hand, and then he just throws it onto the earth. . . . the piece of skin turns into, like, bricks and then people build buildings from it." For Jesse, it is within his imagination that he can begin to reach the image of God. To think that our houses are made of God's skin is, to me, strikingly beautiful. It is, as Jesse says, "awesome, like a recycling spirit to help the humans." In this relationship, Jesse embodies both the wonder of life and the newfound awareness of his particular spirituality taking shape. It is this quality that

I hope my photographs in this book hold. Here photography becomes the medium in which to create a space to talk about God.

A photograph is the viewer's creation as much as it is the subject's and the photographer's. It is a piece of the world that simultaneously exists as that which was once real and that which is memory. The photograph can be a doorway into our own imagination, a mystical door we open and walk through, beyond which lies another world—a world beyond the frame, time, or the limits of what is known about God, but a world that cannot exist without these constraints.

What emerges in the process of photographing people and inquiring about their views of God is that God exists in no one place, not fully in our images nor fully in our words, but among us and in the places between. My wish is that the following pages become a representation of this inquiry. As the portraits and the words come together through the subjects' desires and passions to reveal their faith, God is there. God exists.

Perhaps the meaning of God lies within our efforts, within our search. Is it possible then that God could be defined by each person's individual interpretation, rather than that which is already fully assembled by someone else?

Adam Gaynor

IMAGES
OF GOD

It's a lot of work to be God. He makes the wind and the storms, which make the trees and flowers grow. He's giving love to everybody and making the wings for the angels. God's hardest job is taking care of the kids. This is what makes God really tired. He lies down in the clouds to rest for a few days. If he doesn't rest, God will die and go to Heaven. If that happens, Jesus will take God's job.

MALAIKA

—————.

I reckon the closest thing to praying would be being in harmony with nature and having respect for it. The mountains and the clouds—they were all here, not made by man. There should be some force behind that.

I talked to an old family friend when my grandfather died two years ago. He'd been out quail hunting and said just walking around here in the woods on a Sunday morning is going to church. That's my idea too. Just being in nature—in everything you see here—is the closest thing to praying. With all the trouble you hear about in the world news, it's refreshing to see that there still is nature and unspoiled things around.

LANGLEY

———.

To me, God has so many faces. I think what makes people very uncomfortable about God is to see God as an angry being, something so vicious and evil. Kali is a Hindu goddess who dances on the cremation ground. She is the goddess of death and birth. If something doesn't die, then something new doesn't come into being. I think it's a natural process.

SUSMITA

—————————.

Without tradition, I would feel a certain emptiness in life. Before I was religious, I had a good time and everything was going well, but there was always that certain emptiness that comes from the soul. It's the soul yearning to return to the creator. Every person feels this in different ways. Some people may get depressed. Some may feel like they're not accomplishing anything. Some might go searching in different countries or for different things, but all desires come from the soul and from love. You see, love is really a love for the creator. It's just that we don't channel it to the right places; we have to try to always realize the source the love is coming from. Then we must bring love back to the creator to feel that closeness and that attachment to G—d. It's a beautiful thing to see and practice.

MOSHE

——————.

Jesus is the best friend I've ever had. He's
been my mother; he's been my father. I've
been saved for the past eleven years, and
so far, I have found no fault in serving
God. I have no doubt in my mind that
I'm doing the right thing, no doubt
whatsoever. God protects you from so
many things, maybe from being a thief or
from taking drugs. You're guided away
from these things. You can just leave all
your problems anytime. Just have faith in
him, and he'll see you through. Even
though I feel blessed, it hurts me that my
brothers and sisters aren't saved. I
continue to pray for them because I
know God will save them one day.

H Y A C I N T H

The reason I don't like the word God is that it implies there's something other, something else. There's us, and then there's God. That doesn't reflect my experience. Quakers speak of the inner light. We believe that God is within us. Every event and every person has something in it that teaches or informs us. There is no hierarchy. The community is the church, the minister, and the liturgy. The people you worship with are everything.

Being a Quaker is a very vibrant and powerful experience. Quakers worship in silence, and we can worship anywhere at all. If you have two Quakers together, you can have a Quaker service. We usually get together at what's called "meeting houses." There's no creed. Quakers believe there is God in every person. From that comes the belief in nonviolence and acceptance of everyone. It's really been a spiritual and social home for me.

EILEEN

From all the icons that I've seen, I have a picture of God in my head. He has a beard, but no mustache. He has long, brown hair. He looks like someone in his forties. God's like a person that just lives in the sky. He controls our lives. He gave us life, so we should pay him back. We should help others. We should live our lives and not do drugs and stuff and help people. We shouldn't spend all our time playing. We should think about the future.

When you do something bad, think about it. Pray to God. Say you're sorry, but it's better not to do anything really bad. I pray every night that everything will be fine, that everything is like it is now. Sometimes I even ask him for something like a dog and stuff. I also ask him that nobody has bad dreams. Everybody prays for different things.

TAYA

I think with all the suffering that I've had
in my life, I believe what my mother says,
I'll be in a better place someday—
Heaven. I'm not afraid anymore of dying
from the virus. I just don't want to die in
the gutter. That's what I'm afraid of.

I'm a poor man, okay. But I got clothes
on my back, I got people that love me,
care for me, and I have food to eat every
day. I don't have to go out and steal; I
don't have to go out and hurt anybody to
get that fix in my arm. Maybe God is
letting this happen just to see how really
strong this person is in his beliefs. I know
that God exists, and my belief is that what
happens is for the good of all.

HENRY

God was a word that never made sense to
me. I have no guilt about not believing.
I don't think it's evil not to believe. No,
I really am an atheist. I mean, think about
it. How could there be a God? How
could there be any force that has an
influence on man? If there were, it would
have to be a good force if it were a God,
and how could that be? Look at all the
killing going on, the murdering, the
fighting. Look at the people dying young.
I lost a son when he was nineteen. How
could that happen? Does God exist?
Is God a good person? Just look around.
I don't see how anyone could answer yes.

M I M I

God floats by the side of earth. When his skin falls off, he has it in his hand, and then he just throws it onto the earth. You know how the earth spins? So, like, it goes onto one part of the earth, and then the piece of skin turns into, like, bricks and then people build buildings from it. I think about it, and it's awesome, like a recycling spirit to help the humans.

J E S S E

I will always believe in God, but sometimes I get angry with him.
My family lives in Haiti, and the environment is really hard for them.
I ask myself every day, *Why those people struggling; why those people starving?*
God doesn't change things all of a sudden; it takes time, and God wants you to be patient with him. I believe in that.

CHARNEL

————————.

I can see how bleak life could be without loving something. Like a shepherd wandering in the desert with just a staff and no sheep. I feel that even though tragedy happens, it should never paralyze you from living a happy and full life. Time is so short here. God is not trying to punish us; I don't believe in that.

My dad died in an accident when I was eleven. I miss him terribly, but I have never doubted my faith. How do I explain it? You give that up and then you're left with what? Cold, dark nothing. It comes down to trying to keep as much love in my little personal world as I possibly can. And when I stop to think about how lucky I am, I pray: I hope I don't lose any of this.

PATRICIA

S uffering is mystery. I'm not sure it would help me if I knew the full dimensions of that mystery. I'm not worried about trying to have an answer for everything. I'm pretty content to let God be God. I'm satisfied with what's been revealed. I don't know what God's doing with the whole world or ultimately what someone else's religious experience is. I'm happy to let God understand that.

THE REVEREND MINOR

———————.

The best thing about God is that I can feel his presence all around me. Even working the soil on the farm brings me close with God. He doesn't turn off at night when you do. Before I go to bed, I play the organ. I'm out in the country, so nobody can hear me. It takes all those other things out of my mind, and it really helps me sleep. He's there with me during the night when I play. He's there in the morning when I wake up. I feel him with me all during the day. And I frequently stop during the day to say short prayers. If there is anything bothering me that I would like to talk about, I just speak freely in short prayers.

Look for him in everything around you, because he's there.

M A E

———————.

Every day I'm faced with tragedy, with people labeling me in their minds. Because of the way I'm dressed and the way I look, people will always say that I am a certain type of person according to their understanding, and the understanding right now in America is that anyone who's in Islam or who's a Muslim is this type of person: They think we blow things up, we have no remorse, we're baby killers.

I am a man, and peace is within myself. It has always been in existence, and now I have been able to capture it more and more. Every day of my existence is a chance to grab peace. I believe that all good is from Allah and all evil is from ourselves. Just take a look at the heavens. There are no flaws in the heavens. There are no flaws in nature. The only flaws are in man. And it's not even that he is a flaw, but he is flawed in his own way of living.

Y U S A F

I put my life in God's hands. He created us for his pleasure. We are here so that he can enjoy us and that we can enjoy the beautiful things that he has created for us.

Before you accept God, you are God's creation, but you're not God's child. I don't mean this as a closed-minded statement. You're separated from God by sin, and when you come to that place where you're willing to admit that you are a sinner, you receive. I feel guilty because I'm trying to be perfect when in fact I don't have to be perfect. God's going to love me whether I'm good or bad.

K I M

——————.

All the Navajos in the desert go over there to the cliffs and talk to the Lord. Nobody hears nothing except the snakes and the birds. That's all you got on the reservation. God does everything for us. He makes the fish in the water for you to eat when you got no money. The Lord provides for me because I've got faith, and that makes the Lord happy.

JOE

I think if you don't believe in God, you shouldn't be forced into believing. It's a personal choice. It's not for someone else to make for you. I think I believe in God because of the Bible and what people have taught me. If I were alone in the world, I wouldn't know about these things. I probably wouldn't believe in God. It's because of the teachings through the years and through Sunday school that I do.

You know, though, I think if I were alone on an island, I'm sure I'd find a way to know God. Something might just happen. I might be really desperate and find food and water. Just like a miracle. I would know it came from something else, and I would be thinking, *Thank you, God.*

COREY

———————.

Now how can Jesus Christ, who died upon the cross as a human, come back to life? That is what we call the mystery of the Resurrection. I believe in that, because I have the gift of faith. How can there be one God, and yet be a person in God, and yet not be three Gods? That's the mystery of the Trinity. I cannot understand it. I can talk about it, even though I don't understand it.

Faith is, as Saint Paul teaches us, the belief in what we cannot see. It's also a mystery that we cannot understand. I must make choices that are consistent with my belief in order to sustain and strengthen my faith. The difficulties we have with faith come when we're acting in a way that is contrary to our moral system. Something has to give. Either we discontinue acting in that way, or we compromise our faith.

God is the one who loves me. God is the creator. He assumes a human nature that lives among us and shows us how to live. "He who follows me walks not in darkness. I am the light of the world."

FATHER CHRISTIAN

To be a Buddhist monk is to connect with an ancient tradition that was set up by an enlightened being. This tradition is kept very pure, close to the way it was kept back then. Not many people have the karma to step into the monastic life and to be able to let go of worldly things. There is a lot more impetus to practice, a lot more support and momentum behind me now. Every time I look down, I see this robe that I'm wearing and it reminds me of what I'm representing and how I'm supposed to act. It reminds me to put my ego and my concerns second to that of the dharma. It's letting go of those things with a sense of faith that, when I let go, they will be replaced with a greater sense of happiness and deeper things. And that's kind of a scary aspect: fear of the unknown.

ROHANA

 **W**hen God is not with me, it's because I've left God. God never leaves me.

Instead of going downstream, I headed upstream toward a waterfall. We flipped over. I didn't have time to think about what was happening to me. I got sucked into what's called a hole or a washer. Its strong currents turn around like a washing machine; it just sucks you down in a vicious swirl below the surface. What went through my mind was, Oh no, not now, I'm not ready yet, *and then I thought,* I'm not alone. My God is with me. Whatever my God has in mind for me is okay. *This thought helped me relax my body.*

I was then released, shot down river, and battered against rocks. I was very weak and light-headed. I kept thinking that God was with me and that wherever I might go would be a better place. All of a sudden I got sucked under again. I thought, God must not be so sure what to do with me. I'm not alone; I'm not alone. *I started thinking of nice things, mountains in Wyoming, my beautiful family. I relaxed and got released one more time. I was freezing by now and started to shake, and then I was rescued.*

God is always with me. God is my buddy.

J O

When I was a child living in Jamaica, I thought God rained down milk and honey from heaven. I've been taking care of sick people for fifteen years, and I've watched so many of them take their last breath. I was with a woman one day, a young woman. She had breast cancer and was so afraid of dying. I said, "Talk to me," and she said, "You know, Florence, I'm afraid; I'm afraid of dying. Does it hurt? Is it hard?"

I said, "No, honey, you won't know about it. You're just going to sleep." That's how it is. You take sleep and you mark death. She listened to me, and she was perfect. It calmed her down very good. And you know something? She did sleep. She did sleep and she died, but all that fear went away.

Wherever you're going, you won't be suffering. If we do right, God will be waiting for us with the milk and honey.

FLORENCE

———————.

God was the first one who brought animals to earth. They were the first people. Some think we came from apes. Porcupines came first, then bears. The bears shrunk and became these guys, raccoons. God was supposed to bring animals down so people could be nice to 'em, but all of a sudden it turned out people were mean to them. Run 'em over on purpose. I had a kid in my class who saw a possum while riding on his go-cart. He said, "Let's go run it over!" And they went and ran it over. The possum was dead—like that. I think God will send 'em to Hell. He should if he doesn't.

When the animals die, they become God's pets as angels. And once all the animals die, what are we gonna do? People are going to say to their kids, "Oh, once there was animals here." And then children are going to be, like, "But where are they now?"

LISA

I try to have the Torah govern my life in a way that gives my life meaning and purpose. I know that most of my communication to G—d is limited to the synagogue, but I know that G—d's communication to me is also every breath, every sight, and every thought. These are all forms of prayer, even though we don't realize it at times. Does G—d communicate back to us? I think the answer is yes. I'm in touch with who I really am and the part of G—d within me. You just have to understand the language of G—d, and that's what the studying of the Torah is: how God's language is spoken in the world and in one's life experience. To me, that's a tremendous joy.

MATIS

I believe it's possible that being here may be just a matter of existence with no real purpose. So what do other people do to make themselves sleep easy? They turn the complex question into a profound answer. They invent that there's a big man on top, and he is the one who has set everything up, and don't worry, he has a purpose, just have faith. I think that's fine for a lot of people, but I prefer to engage the complex questions, and religion rules that out.

JULES

———————.

When you're a child, clearly you believe in God. You know, every night you say your prayers and you believe in God. Then as events in your life become traumatic, and you pray and nothing happens, you start thinking, *Well, that's no God.* I was in a concentration camp. How could that not help but change my idea of God?

Wars have been caused by religion, and they were fought in a height of passion. People passionately believed in something, and they fought for it. With the Nazis, it was different. This was cold-blooded, scientifically designed murder. Clearly God is not just, and there is no justice in God's rulings and makings. That's definite. Where is he in all this world's happenings? I ask this not just because of my own experience in the concentration camps, but because of all the innocent people who died.

MARIANNE

It's probably one of the things in religion that is very close to the truth. There's this thing called faith, and in order to find faith, you have to have the absurd. If everything was beautiful and wonderful, faith would not exist. Everything is the way it should be. That's why God is so big. God can actually understand and see what's going on and yet not take part in changing it. We have trees and growth to see that life exists, and I think that faith is the life God can see. Faith is a tree for God.

PHILIP

——————.

Y ou're taught to love people, to be kind, to be morally good. How do you comprehend it, then, when you're told as a child that you can't play with a friend because her father doesn't want his daughter to play with someone of a different religion? How can you be told to go to services and to pray to God when you go to school the next day with kids who go to church, yet are so discriminating against you? I couldn't live with that.

I think, in some ways, that has been my experience with religion. It makes me feel ashamed in some ways. Your religion and your connection with God is also part of your identity. You should be proud of that. It isn't something that you should hide, like I have. I feel sad about that.

E L Y S A

People use God because they have no one to talk to, and it gives them faith. I think God doesn't really exist, but other kids believe in God because their parents believe in it. The kids always think if their parents believe in it, it's probably what's true. They're adults and they know everything. But if people didn't have a God to talk to, everyone would lose faith and go out and do anything they wanted to. The whole world would just be a bunch of drunk people lying everywhere, and everyone would be upset, killing people and everything. Something is wrong if people have faith in God and yet they still do horrible things.

ANNA

Our only barriers are the barriers of our own minds, our egos. It's very easy to think in terms of self-centeredness, and to give that up is not easy. I think there's a fear of annihilation that comes from giving up the little self.

Zazen is a form of meditation, a quiet sitting. It's really a quieting of all the noise that goes on in our heads. If we can stop our thinking for a while and start fresh, we see that the things that bother us aren't that bad or intense. As we practice more and more, we realize that there's a great joy that comes when we can lose the little self. It allows us to experience our true nature, and it's a joyful thing. Just to give yourself completely to a beautiful bird singing—like that. When you let go of yourself, there's only that wonderful birdsong; that's all there is. It fills the universe.

BILL

Sometimes when I'm alone and in my room, I feel like there's someone there. And I think that it's one of my relatives that died, or God, or someone in Heaven that I can't see. It makes me feel happy that people that have died actually go to Heaven. I feel comfort in that because I don't really want to die; I don't want to die at all. I want to believe that my soul is still going to be alive. It makes me so scared that, if I didn't believe in him, then I would really be scared of dying. Believing makes me feel that I'm not alone.

SARAH 'ROSE

———————.

God's a good spirit. When he looks down, he sees if anything's wrong or if anything bad's happening. I know that he's a good spirit because it looks so calm in the skies. You know how clouds take the shape of pictures and things? God lives in the sky, and the reason you can't see him is because he blends into the clouds. You have to look up really hard because a cloud can take the shape of anything. When it's starting to rain or the clouds get dark, he tries to clear it up. That's how I see him, and when the sun shines down because the heavens are opening, he's doing that. His spirit is part of all of us, even the bad people who don't really care. His spirit disappears in them. He's still trying to put it back in and turn them back into good people.

S T E P H E N

———————.

God to me is all-in-one God. Anything that has the essence of life is of God. A blade of grass. A grasshopper. Anything that carries the light of living in itself is the spirit of God. I see God as a single cell, and we're many pieces to it. We've just forgotten. I don't think a blade of grass has forgotten, nor anything beyond the human form, because it always lives in the present moment. And being in the present moment is knowing you are of the essence of God.

I'm a believer in reincarnation, that when we are of nonphysical form, we are a part of God. We make a choice to come back to the school of earth and accept that we will forget what has happened before. Hopefully, in that short life span of time, we work toward remembering again who we are and what we are.

I think I have lived thousands and thousands of lives. I've been a blade of grass, as much as I believe I've been Hercules. I've lived all lives. And at the same time, I've forgotten all of them. I have come back here to try and not only remember, but to teach—to show the way.

KATHY

The beauty of Allah is basically in your heart. This world would be nothing without Allah. He is the one who will take care of everything, and he is the only one who makes the decisions. He has taken care of everything before you were born, and he will take care of everything at the end. And that is a promise.

TARIQ

———————.

I've always believed in God, but I feared him as a child. My mom used to say that if I didn't pray to God or talk to him, I was going to go to Hell, or my soul would be condemned. Now, I believe in God out of habit, not because I feel him in my soul. I should feel not mad about this, but not so comfortable either. I should be able to live by the religion that I want and not what my parents taught me. Maybe I want to believe in God in a different way. Maybe I don't feel God like a Catholic would or like I did as a child. I think parents should use other words than mine did to tell their children to do the right thing about God.

OMAR

Y ou're less likely to hurt all of creation if you don't interpret what they're doing in personal terms. You're less likely to take advantage of someone if you're not living in constant fear and preoccupation with, How do I get enough? How do I make myself safe? *We hit on these things that are supposed to somehow save us. For some people it's money or power, and they can never get enough. For some it's love, or even less acceptable things like drugs. We try to block out that fear in one way or another. If you are facing that fear instead, which you can do with practice, you don't run from it. You learn to tolerate it. Not easy.*

Meditation is a lifelong process. As one follows a course of Zen practice very seriously for a long period of time, the preoccupation with the ego, or self, loosens. When that happens, one's treatment of all other creatures, not just human beings, tends to be far more beneficial.

DONNA

The devil is red and has horns. He lives in places where there's fire. First he was in Heaven, but he started being bad, so then God had to send him down out of Heaven.

If you don't be good, you might be worshiping the devil. They say that God gets angry when you're bad. It doesn't matter where you are. Even under the water. He knows. It starts to thunder and lightning when he is mad, and when you do well in the world, he's very happy. He makes a shiny day.

L A U R E N

After recovering from a stroke, I was worried whether I was going to be able to finish my life's work, which is to document the history of this church. Our church is a national shrine today. That occurred in the fifties, when the church was restored to its seventeenth-century appearance. We have the oldest intact English chamber organ in the world. It was built in the early sixteenth century. I know so much history about this church that nobody else knows, and it's not written down anywhere. I'm afraid that when I'm gone, it will be gone.

The church has been very important to me ever since I was a little child. I don't know if I can explain it. It's just a building; I know that. But it's God's house, and even though there are no longer people here on a regular basis, I'm here every day. When I walk into the building, I see and feel something each time that I've never experienced before. I feel the presence of all the people who have been here before. I feel God shining through.

DICK

It's frightening to come to the revelation that there's a Hell and there's a Heaven. There is a fork in the road at the end of life. Some will go up, and some will go down. One of the most important things I want to do is to see how many people I can help by letting them know there's a better way. There's no higher calling in life—none that's more important—than being a minister, or sharing the life message that Jesus offers. Jesus is the answer. Jesus is the Truth, the Light, and the Way. And no man goes to the Father except through him. That's what God wants for us. He wants us to love him with all of our hearts, with all of our minds, and with all of our souls.

DAVE

————————.

Sometimes when things happen to me, I get a little mad at God. I blame God. If I get really, really hurt, I'll say, "I hate you, God," but I don't mean it. Have you ever gotten really mad and wanted to kill somebody? That's happened to me millions of times. I'll say, "God, please help me," and after, like, ten minutes, he'll cool me down. I believe that God is a really powerful energy of light, and bad energy is dark like the devil, and light overpowers dark any day.

C . J .

I'm not the praying kind. Maybe I feel
unfulfilled or something, like I'm a
shallow person because I don't believe in
God. I really never thought about it.
Maybe I wish I could have some faith. It
gives people a lot of comfort, and I could
use that comfort. I just can't go through
that procedure of saying, "Yes, I believe,"
when I really don't. Maybe I'm afraid to
get involved for fear it might not work
out. And then you say to yourself, *Gee,
I'm all alone, and yet I didn't allow myself to
get involved.* So it's a torment.

J O H N

I have a friend in school, and she does not believe in Heaven. Me and Molly tried to get her to believe in Heaven. We said, "Do you believe in God?" She said, "Yes." "Then you believe in Heaven or else where does God live? Is he homeless?" She still doesn't believe in Heaven and her name is Paige. She even slapped Molly on the cheek once. It bothers me a little because I don't want God to be homeless.

RACHEL

―――――――.

When I was a little girl, I had a dream. My grandfather came to me and explained that he was dying. He described a pale blue light the color of the sea. I pictured his soul floating with wings. That next morning he died. The sea always reminds me of him.

E R I K A

The basic principle of G—d is that we cannot conceive of him fully. A person can learn for one hundred years and still not get to his fullest capacity of understanding G—d. We believe there are seven general galaxies in the world and to walk each galaxy takes five hundred years. But that's a physical stance. Spiritually, there's also seven worlds. G—d is in all of these worlds, and he's in this world, which is the lowest world. It could take so many years to learn each world and what it represents, physically and spiritually.

We also believe a Jew has a Jewish soul in addition to the regular soul. We believe this. We feel it. The more mitzvoth and study you do, especially of Jewish mysticism, the more your soul will be revealed. As a rabbi, I feel the beauty of it all is the true relationship I have with G—d. It's not something you just feel once a week or on a holiday. It's a connection in which I feel G—d in my life all day long.

RABBI ZUCKER

I will not join any organized religion or faith. That wouldn't bring me closer to God. I used to feel lonely on this path I have chosen until I learned that, through music, I have direct contact with God. For me, this is my own church, temple, or religion. It brings a great harmony of peace to my inner self.

P E I

———————.

Without having a Bible, without having organized religion, priests, and churches, the animal kingdom has an incredible religion that they practice on a daily basis with each other. I think God did a better job with animals than he did with people. There are so many ways that animals interact and relate to each other that are far better, more peaceful, and more cooperative than humans. I don't know whether greed ever has to be factored into their world. When they kill, it's to kill what they eat. It is, in fact, only domesticated dogs who kill just for the sport of killing. Humans do the same.

There's got to be some sort of mitigation for the damage that greed and evil causes if we're going to salvage the creation that God has given us. Otherwise we may be looking at the day it all gets destroyed, and for us to be the cause of that destruction is something I don't personally want to get involved in. This is the reason I dedicate my life to wildlife and marine rescue work.

RICK

I connect with the Divine through the study of astrology. The correlation of planetary movement to our actual experiences is profound and beyond logic. Astrology helps us interpret how the Divine operates in our lives through the convergence of fate and free will in a way that gives meaning to experience. Through astrology, a universal wisdom is revealed that some call God. This cosmic consciousness permeates all layers of existence in a way that is not intellectually understandable but is as real and tangible as the words that I am speaking.

In the twenty-four years I have been an astrologer, I've seen how planetary symbols reveal the meaning of experiences that otherwise would be incomprehensible. If we can extract meaning out of a difficult situation, we can find peace and go on. Astrology enables us to develop a close personal relationship to the Divine, and when we do that, we each stay true to our own unique essential nature.

NICKI

My view about religion is that you shouldn't start it as a kid. What does a kid know? Everybody says, "I want my kids to go to church or temple." I say, "Keep religion away from people until they're about eighteen," because for me, religion is an adult's business, not a kid's. It's too easy to get brainwashed as a kid, and you do things although you don't know why, but you feel bad if you don't.

Buddhism is great because there's no sin. I mean, you can be stupid; there's stupidity. And we are stupid. I mean, the first noble truth is "Life is suffering." And it is. Shit is all around, and there's no escaping it, but it doesn't have to be made worse and worse. The second truth is that the cause of suffering is our own attachment to self. All ego. So Buddhism is about the annihilation of ego. Buddhism is accepting oneself as one is, rather than trying to imagine oneself as some kind of very different person. That's the point.

GORDON

I guess I'll never forget how many people actually gave their lives to Christ and to God. The fact that war has brought a lot more people closer to God is a good thing. If war has to bring about peace, then that's what you have to do.

We were really scared in the Gulf War, and it did humble a lot of people. Prayer, we all felt, was the answer. I prayed a lot. I even prayed for the Iraqi people. I know God is going to do something much better to help get me through this, so the soldiers and I hold on to that faith. Being at war has brought me closer to God.

GARY

The world situation bothers me: the racism, the violence. My dream would be to somehow open up the hearts in the world and put in compassion as a way of life. Then we would feel the appreciation of the planet and of each other.

How come there are so many problems in the world if so many people believe in God? Because we believe in God doesn't mean we're perfect. I think that problems exist because of free will and human weakness. I think we're easily blinded with greed and selfishness and navel gazing, that we cause our own problems. And I do think trying to journey with God is an ideal. Yet if we've chosen to take that fundamental journey with God, we're going to take three steps forward, one step back. People struggle with that.

SISTER DAMIAN

I don't feel bad for people who don't believe in God. I don't think anyone should be mad because they worship something else or don't believe in a guy who's invisible. I think it's not God's fault, it's their fault. They should help themselves. God can't focus on one thing. It's the people who choose to fight over stupid things, like the Christians who wanted to fight with the Jews because they didn't like them. I mean, the Nazis, not the Christians, were fighting with the Jewish people, and you should have seen what they were doing to them. God couldn't prevent that. It's not his fault.

God doesn't make people a certain way. God can never be bad. Never. 'Cause if he is a God, then why would he be bad? He was chosen because he can help people.

SARA

I t is often surprising to others that I do not feel the need to worship God with a group in any organized ritual. I prefer to think that, as God is a part of me that dwells within, I can commune with him in a meditative state whenever the spirit moves me. This is my shared personal connection with God, but I believe he is anywhere and everywhere we choose to seek him, be it in a cathedral or in an open field. I have chosen the way to him that gives me peace, that offers guidance, protection, and, above all else, love.

GEAN

————————.

I can't imagine or comprehend not believing in God. When I was younger, I thought about being a minister. I wanted to go to Heaven and be with my grandmother; yet ministers, even the preachers in the Pentecostal church, talked about homosexuality being a sin, and there I was, no way out. I was terribly confused because it was something I didn't want to be. It would have been tragic if I had killed myself because of the way I was made to feel, the embarrassment my family felt. Then, I thought suicide was a quicker way to burn in Hell.

The best thing about God now is that I'm accepted the way I am, and I'm loved just like this.

FREDRICK

—————.

For sure God is good. My mom says that God lives between people and when people are good to each other, then God is good. When people aren't good, maybe God is just sleeping. God gets tired because people have so many problems. He doesn't like to wake up sometimes because there are so many people that need him. That's why he's sleeping all the time. Maybe he got mad that people don't take care of each other better.

If I saw God, I would ask him, "How come no one can see you anymore?"

E L I Z A

To be a monk isn't just to be like a book, carrying on a tradition and form. You have to embody your role. Tradition is part of that role, but I don't think it's the ultimate responsibility for me. I chose the path Buddha shared with the world because I felt like it was the most conducive lifestyle for meditation and freedom from suffering. It's not about stopping feelings from arising. It's about seeing them in their right perspective and letting them go.

We don't listen to music or indulge in sense pleasures, though we still have eyes, and we still have ears and tongues. You can't stop those from receiving pleasant feelings, but when you start planning to experience, you start identifying yourself with that experience. That's when suffering arises. If fear, for example, does arise in my mind, I just see it as fear, and I don't necessarily identify it as myself. If you have sufficient wisdom and understanding of fear, a lot of all fear, cravings, and anger won't arise.

PUNNA

I feel that sometimes I'm alone because nobody feels the way I do. You can't understand the Bible until you're born again. People are not happy in churches because they haven't been saved. The Bible says if you confess your sins, God is faithful and just to forgive you your sins. He cleanses us from all unrighteousness.

The Lord deals with you like you deal with your children. When your kids are small, you keep telling your children not to do something, and you explain why. And if they keep on doing it, you know, you're going to whip them. And that's the way it is with the Lord. If you're not serving him and doing what he wants you to do, then you're no good on this earth. Sometimes he just takes you on to Heaven to complete your maturity.

J O   A N N

The way humans place themselves above every other living thing I find to be a disrespect, almost an ignorance. Karma is innately important. The cycle of life and nature, the way we all relate and affect each other, is more of a spirituality than a God. Spirituality is based in human beings and all living things living together for the good of the planet and our lives. I think that's ultimately it, that everything is connected spiritually and by souls.

Human beings always want to be able to have something tangible to lock on to. I'm not taking meaning away from the Bible or other religious documents, but instead of following a set of rules and stories telling how to live life, I see it as more of a mystery—we don't have all the answers.

CASSANDRA

The most important thing about God, to me, is that he died on the cross for everyone in the world, not just for me. He loves everyone and also really helps you out. I think he helps me in every way. I used to always be scared that there was a bogeyman under my bed. I would always leave the lights on. I would pray because I was really, really scared. After I prayed, I was still scared but not as much. It really helped. He's inside of us and loves us and wants to help everyone, not just certain kinds of people. He makes me feel more comfortable inside.

M E R E D I T H

———————.

FONG: *The world is Heaven and Hell. In China, I was always thinking that we should have a God to take care of us The bombs fell there every day. Our house was bombed. Our friends were killed. In my heart, I was always praying to God for the fighting to stop between the Japanese and the Chinese. I prayed for people to have food and for the killing to stop. I pray to God and to Saint Mary to help me out during my journey through life. God has been with me all this time. I know that I am very lucky that I didn't get killed. Thank you, God. Thank you.*

STEPHEN: Looking back, it bothers me that God allowed such destruction. Ever since I was born it's been war, war, war. I know God wants to help us overcome our difficulties. One way of achieving this, to me, is to pray. I've always prayed. I pray in three different languages. Every day I thank God before I go to bed that I'm not in the situation I used to be when I was growing up. I was poor. I had not one penny to spend. Almost every day my stomach was growling and grinding. Today I have a good life. We have been married for over forty years, and now we have plenty.

There are a lot of people who don't believe in God, like those in early Russia. They didn't believe in God; that's why the country collapsed. Stalin—do you know how many millions of people he had killed? Same with Mao Tse-tung. Look at the Khmer Rouge. Cambodia is a Buddhist country and Pol Pot's regime killed millions of Cambodians. Why? He didn't believe in God. Buddhists don't kill. If more people believed in God, this world would be a better place for us to be in. God is kind. God is compassionate and encourages everyone to be good and compassionate. Love your neighbor like you love yourself.

FONG: *You talk too much!*

STEPHEN AND FONG

It's all black, and there are stars. God's house looks like a big igloo. One day God was swimming around in space collecting space rocks to build his home on Venus. When he went out a little too low, the gravity from Earth sucked him in. He landed in Florida and hit the ground really hard and died. His spirit floated up to Heaven, and he sank into the ground, and all the sand went over him. That's how he got buried. He didn't cry because he's God, and he doesn't like it when other people cry because that's for babies.

In Heaven, he makes people, and then they produce other babies. It's not hard being God because he tells things what to do, and they do it. He tells, like, Mother Earth to spring the flowers and for the clouds to make rain. The best thing about God is that he made me.

D A V I D

ABOUT THE AUTHOR

Adam Gaynor is a New York photographer who specializes in documentary portraiture. His first book, *Portraits of Recovery*, documents those who are in the process of recovering from alcohol and other drug addiction. His new book, *Images of God*, is a series of portraits of people from a wide range of cultures, pondering the universal question of, and more specifically their relationships with and to, the meaning of God.

These photographs were taken over a two-year period throughout most of the eastern coast of the United States. From large cities such as New York, Charlotte, and Miami, to small rural towns like High View, West Virginia; Monk's Corner, South Carolina; and Islamorada, Florida, these photographs and accompanying interviews explore individuals' diverse beliefs of God.

These black-and-white photographs are atmospheric and revealing, posed yet unpretentious. Gaynor's technique is ever changing yet classical and truly seeks to portray his subjects honestly.

Gaynor has a bachelor's degree in special education and has done graduate work at the International Center of Photography. He has taught photography to learning-disabled children and now dedicates his time to fine art and commercial work.

Gaynor can be contacted at his Web site: www.adamgaynor.com

Photo by Elsa Li'Donni

HAZELDEN INFORMATION AND EDUCATIONAL SERVICES is a division of the Hazelden Foundation, a not-for-profit organization. Since 1949, Hazelden has been a leader in promoting the dignity and treatment of people afflicted with the disease of chemical dependency.

The mission of the foundation is to improve the quality of life for individuals, families, and communities by providing a national continuum of information, education, and recovery services that are widely accessible; to advance the field through research and training; and to improve our quality and effectiveness through continuous improvement and innovation.

Stemming from that, the mission of this division is to provide quality information and support to people wherever they may be in their personal journey—from education and early intervention, through treatment and recovery, to personal and spiritual growth.

Although our treatment programs do not necessarily use everything Hazelden publishes, our bibliotherapeutic materials support our mission and the Twelve Step philosophy upon which it is based. We encourage your comments and feedback.

The headquarters of the Hazelden Foundation are in Center City, Minnesota. Additional treatment facilities are located in Chicago, Illinois; New York, New York; Plymouth, Minnesota; St. Paul, Minnesota; and West Palm Beach, Florida. At these sites, we provide a continuum of care for men and women of all ages. Our Plymouth facility is designed specifically for youth and families.

For more information on Hazelden, please call **1-800-257-7800**. *Or you may access our World Wide Web site on the Internet at* **http://www.hazelden.org.**